Ways to Build a Roadblock

Ways to Build a Roadblock
Josh Ekroy

ISBN: 978-0-9927589-0-5

Copyright © Josh Ekroy, 2014

Cover photograph © Eleanor Bennett
www.eleanorleonnebennett.zenfolio.com

All rights reserved. No part of this work may be reproduced, stored or transmitted in any form or by any means, graphic, electronic, recorded or mechanical, without the prior written permission of the publisher.

Josh Ekroy has asserted his right under Section 77 of the Copyright, Designs and Patents Act 1988 to be identified as the author of this work.

First published May 2014 by:

Nine Arches Press
PO Box 6269
Rugby
CV21 9NL

www.ninearchespress.com

Printed in Britain by:
imprintdigital.net
Seychelles Farm,
Upton Pyne,
Exeter
EX5 5HY
www.imprintdigital.net

Ways to Build a Roadblock

Josh Ekroy

Nine
Arches
Press

new poets series

Josh Ekroy was born in Essex, brought up in Surrey and educated in Sussex and Kentish Town. In another life he wrote novels for which the world was not yet ready as well as humorous articles which appeared in magazines including *Punch*. He now lives next to a lot of building sites in the City of London. He taught English for some years mainly in FE Colleges and for two years in Kiribati in the Pacific, which was then and is now disappearing beneath the waves as ocean levels rise. His poems appear in magazines, anthologies and webzines. *Ways to Build a Roadblock* is his first collection.

CONTENTS

I

From the golfcart	9
Ways to Build a Roadblock	10
My rifle	11
Achilles in Helmand	12
Brotherhood	14
SAMs	15
Barracks Snorers	16
Guided Tour	17
Hephaestus	19
Saddam Hussein's Overbite Speaks	20
Uncurling the Human	21
The stone in me	22
Babur's Tulips	23
Like dense cotton and it started to burn	24
Disinterested	25
Pause	26

II

78rpm	29
Langtree, April	30
First Woodpecker	31
Goldfinches	32
Musical Vienna – A Guided Tour	33
Gothic Aunt Revival	34
Sheep and Poetry	35
The Colour of Memory	36
Shostakovich 5	37
Rafah	38
Kafka's Recipe for Boiled Cabbage	40

Vote Pine Tree	42
Vote Horse	43
Lord Hutton Reports	44
R&R	45
Shades	46
Chapter VII	47
Owls	49
Sleeper Cell	50
Ted Smith	51

III

Recruitment	55
Cellar	56
Tourist Bus Halt	57
Rehearsing The Anopheles Play	58
In A Supply Tunnel, Rafah	59
Flight	61
Some Useful Phrases	63
Sniffer Patrol	64
Camp X-Ray	65
The Restroom	66
Medical Advances	67
Waiting for the Americans	68
The Agony	69
Imminent Release	71
The Trojan Enquiry	72
Camp No	74
Leader	75
Orange	76
Elegy	77
Acknowledgements	81
Acknowledgements of Sources	82

I

From the Golfcart

In some species of Empid Fly,
the male presents the female
with a slaughtered insect.
While she is occupied in eating it
he can mate her, small as he is,
without fear of being eaten himself.

When Blair visits Bush at Crawford in 2003
there's a slight frown disfiguring Blair's grin
as he waves to the crowd. But Bush
has the look of a man who can take corners
at speed. He tells the press,
Tony might be more nuanced than me.

Ways to Build a Roadblock

You can throw a cross-wire at windscreen height,
or a length of sisal rope; you can place
rusty oil drums in the road or construct
cairns of volcano boulders. Shattered glass,
nails will suffice, or sapless thorn branches.
Wreaths of stapelia and cycad trunks
can't be overrun. But the surest way
is to use a tall wardrobe. It should have
a mirror which you angle to the sun
to dazzle any road-user. They'll halt
a good way off and walk, frowning perhaps,
towards you, acting normal. Air's heated
to whiteness and vibrates above the road
like boiling water. Your visitor will
hold his breath, listen to the cicadas,
whose harsh rattles accuse, then deafen him.
Slow, you emerge from your palm tree shadow,
wait for him to greet you. If he uses
the wrong word, at once set him to work
to dig his own grave. He utters the right
one: you will both repeat it many times,
passing it back and forth like a grenade.

My rifle

Throws jelly beans to shouting boys.
Reveals what intimacy means.
Plays *The Song of the Earth* to swooning ladies.
Never blames anyone.

My rifle wears a bespoke suit.
Delivers non-violent outcomes.
Outshines the suns on my brassards.
Fishes in the cross-hairs for semiquavers.

Sometimes my rifle's a wowser.
Wins true hearts and deep minds
then calls me slattern and laughs in a friendly manner.
Doesn't like to ride shotgun.

My rifle's a strict tonometer.
Is my refresher towelette.
Draws graffiti in the pargeting.
Loves the silver prose of Ruskin.

My rifle whistles up the dogs.
Is a big softie. Costs nothing.
Endows me with autarky.
Chews the fat with Ministers of Grace.

My rifle came along when I was a kid.
Was softer than nanny.
Charmed bullfinches
from the tip of the larch.

Gives me an appetite.
Like reptiles, it cannot yawn.

Achilles in Helmand

My tent stinks of goatskin.
Stuck here since the Scimitar track
uncogged in the Garmsir fire-fight.
The thump of Agamemnon's drum
was a dodgy Chinook blade.
Waited out two hours under fire, then
lifted back to Lashkar Gar.

Equipment returned a working tank
which couldn't get into reverse
without restarting the engine.
Drops were a joke, the wrong spares
or none at all.

On leave, Briseis didn't get a rise out of me,
hard to remember
her face in the half light,
the folds of her slip falling.

Volunteered for a second tour.

A quarter of Mastiff armoured vehicles
out of action as of 00.00 hours
when I come on duty,
suspensions like shitting concrete.

Pte Patroclus and a couple of newly-recruited Myrmidons
hit an IED –
a shower of crimson rain across the metal road
at the recapture of Musa Qaleh.

Nothing to do but stare at the Euxine Babes video.

My shield's a reinforced Land Rover,
sand in the carburettor,
graffiti on the nearside door.

Brotherhood

At first sight I love him so much
I have him well beaten up. Gilgamesh
totters then disappears beneath a scrum
of enlisted men. We quickly rack him
to the ground, pin him, pull up his shirt,
take turns smacking his stomach as smartly
as we can. I spit on my hot hand first,
spread phlegm, so it will sting the sharpest.

We stand him back on his bare feet.
Specs askew, he brushes dirt
and shakes his roughened
head, blurts out a crimson-faced laugh.

I tell him: *The soldier I love the most*
I beat the worst. A solitary will
sooner or later place me in danger,
but now – this is brotherhood. We hunger
to kill Humbaba for buddies' sakes,
we will not cut off his head and limbs
for patriotism. We'll barbecue
him with our heat-seekers because we know
if we go alone into the cedar forest
where he waits in his lair
he will surely slaughter us one by one.

He looks at me with dull eyes,
praises my candour; leaves it to freeze.
We survey my shivering candour.

SAMs

The moon I recognise from covers
of children's stories is high tonight,
a dusty river-bed grins back.
Dazzling yellow rope-tricks
follow us devotedly where we thud.

Now you people understand
the ejection seat can amputate
if things don't work just perfect,
so slip over the side like you really
don't want to wake the wife.

Next thing I'm out there sky-hiking
with backpack and trying to persuade
a dreamy hand to jerk the pull-ring.
At fifteen thousand feet it happens automatically,
smack, an orange plume
streaming out of my shoulder blades.
Dignified descent out of endless pale,
a need to ask forgiveness.
Rough caps of farm-hands
tilt to reveal foreheads,
I can hear them calling. Words bounce
and steer, elongated by the contours
of the fresh-smelling land.
Springtime.

Barracks Snorers

I wake at three a.m., shift my weight
onto my back; did I hear a storm?
I listen, realise how the snared beat
of their engines has hijacked my dreams.
I've travelled to their rhythms, wrestled
with the hooting agents of their junta,
seen their air-grabs and misfired missiles.
I lie there, stilled by their bluster,
– is that Shostakovich giving birth? –
jump at a snort of indignation, give a start
at the rallying whistles of breath,
the after-loss of freighted effort.

These blokes are nothing like this
when awake; they claim life stands
at ease before them, and though their eyes
deny they've anything to defend,
here they attack, pause, struggle.
How deeply they commit to sleep,
how primally they appeal from it, wriggling
their feet, playing cavemen's pipes.
Their pith is dragged from them in fits,
wheezed air bellowsed out in pangs,
teasing and snagging the glottis,
the stored discourse of dry tongues.

Guided Tour

Come with me my friend, come English,
mind your step in this street, he is Shia,
no-one can move him. The Mujahideen want
him to rot in front of his family
in his dirty tracksuit and broken sandals.
Look how those women turn from the dried blood.

The Shia are cunning and have thicker blood,
Sunnis have hooded eyes and move, English,
with their feet flapping their sandals.
Look at that man, he is certainly a Shia,
you can tell from his shouting family.
Now we leave Mu'alemeen Street. If you want

to visit this morgue, you will also want
a nose tissue because there is stink of blood.
Forty bodies come in – three families.
They have been tortured and dumped, English,
sometimes in the sewage plant, the Shias
float in that black canal with rotting sandals.

The mourners also are attacked, their sandals
stolen too, so their restless fingers want
the cool steel of triggers when they leave Shia
area because they have bad blood
towards Sunni. Behind these blast blocks, English,
they see who is friend, who is family.

Here at this barred window, whole families
lean over shoulders, count sandals.
Look, come here. You can see the clerk, English,
with computer, he does not really want
to show on his screen the pools of blood
for these people at the bars, the Shia.

Come, you can see the dead faces of the Shia
if you stand on your toes – that family
is all wiped out – you can observe black blood
and purple bruises and the tattered sandal.
Come, there is a beggar who is never free from want,
and here are the kids with pistols, English!

The English – do they like to take care of family?
Shia is shamed, if they do not. Remove sandals,
this Mosque wants it. Now we are one blood.

Hephaestus

It is true arsenicosis has taken hold,
my feet are back to front
and I have to lope on a crutch.
But where would Hermes be without
his winged helmet and sandals,
his Airborne Early Warning System?
Or Agamemnon his staff of office,
his Ground-Based Interceptor,
the thrones in the palace of Olympus?

I'm the only one to have been exiled
from heaven and returned.
The gods get into bed with my team,
are entertained by my sweeteners.
At the races we dine them, bond
with games of paint-ball in Arcadia.

Would it be so splendid to rid the world
of the Sea-Sparrow, Tomahawk,
rust-proof sword and Sidewinder?
To how many blacksmiths
do I give employment? What
is family? It is the community
of fire-power.

My revenge against my mother for rejecting me:
I made her a magical golden throne.
Once she was graciously seated,
there Hera stuck.

Saddam Hussein's Overbite Speaks

We had only two minutes of fame when mandible
was forced to admit tongue compressor. But canines
and molars, probed for gold-capped patterns,
disclosed the true identity with a compelling smile.

We loved Iraq which boasted an expert dental service
free to all Iraqis. Nevertheless we in the overbite
are misaligned with those in the underbite
which occludes at jaw base to the front of us.

We could not help but recede, attached
as we are to bone and therefore bonded
into position. After the hanging we remained
loyal to blue lips and choked larynx which

uttered patriotic commands, minted apt sayings,
engulfed so many banquets of larks' tongues.

Uncurling the Human

Make sure all your movements
are as gentle as ferns.
Have some food ready
for when it has unclenched:
warm milk, pigeons' eggs, asparagus tips.
Rock it tenderly as you would
a fear-soiled leveret or a gnat
whose agility has outstripped
itself. Eventually it should raise
its nose. Let it smell the milk:
see the nostrils dilate with all the
deliberation of a caterpillars' progress.
Keep rocking it.
Speak cushions to it. You can warble,
if you wish, as bullfinches do
when they sense no danger. The arms
should start to appear. This is a beautiful
moment but be careful - and never
hold one by a leg: the downpour of blood
scorches the brain causing it to writhe
and creak like a gate. Remove the bold
rivieras of your paws and it will
unbend. Now it should be flat
on its face on the table.
Most are roadkill, but a live one
will be full of maggots and fleas
so disinfect with your phlegm
before you go any further.

THE STONE IN ME

The stone in me speaks directly into the eyes of the toad.
Will make a cute remark about the coffin to the widow.
Tries and fails to lose the sphagnum.
Offers the messenger a drink and only then does he shoot him.

The stone in me derides the knife in the belt.
Pats the hangman on the back, then hangs back.
Plumbs the depths of my boot.
Blows through heat to make mortar shells.

The stone in me rolls in the sand with an air-punch.
Dreams up the slogan, *Coagulation of the Thrilling*.
Denies having been at the scene of remission.
Snaps the heap on someone's cellphone.

Points my barrel at blessings.
Speaks for England though I'm not it.
Beefs up the volume when things go slack.
Bakes pies from memory's crust.

The stone in me is always prompt.
Jostles the scree outside the cave.
Reads snuff porn on the road out of Sangin.
As the years pass, distils an innocence.

Babur's tulips

we fringe the skirts of the mountains' peat meadows
heads agreeing with the brisk winds –
Babur commands that our varieties be counted –
we're thirty-three, including the rose-scented
and the nine-hundred-leaved – he loves death's faces –
velveteen-armed boys – black nazwar –
harram to Sunnis' unsaved souls – but we are not harram –
– us he gives to catamites in token of his immortal lust –
our stamens shape his passion – mad, he carries two men –
runs – one on each shoulder through us up the slope –
from human heads he makes stately pillars –
we salaam to corpses in the downpours

LIKE DENSE COTTON AND IT STARTED TO BURN

There is no need for an investigation.
Some older patients with routine burn patterns
and which are clearly survivable
are alleged to be dying unexpectedly.

Some older patients with routine burn patterns
have been hit by phosphorus shells and
are alleged to be dying unexpectedly.
It starts with small scorches. Young people also

have been hit by phosphorus shells and
in hours the wound becomes impacted.
It starts with small scorches. Young people also
die rapidly and for no obvious reason.

In hours the wound becomes impacted,
there's an odour from those collaterals who have
died rapidly and for no obvious reason.
Toxic fumes emerge from tissue as is normal.

There's an odour from those collaterals who have
dense burning substances which are extracted.
Toxic fumes emerge from tissue as is normal,
flare, then disappear harmlessly.

Dense burning substances which are extracted,
and which are clearly survivable,
flare, then disappear harmlessly.
There is no need for an investigation.

Disinterested

He concedes his French is capable of improvement,
as is the non-nuclear agenda. Yet there persists

moderate faith in a world which doubts his usefulness
and wages war on transparency. To a conflict zone,

the Special Envoy for Genocide will be dispatched
whose report is not yet ready. Surprise may hoist

the eyebrows in order to note who emulates them.
The serious smile has turned others blank

with the knowledge of his probity. Banquets must
be attended on Food Security: beef or mutton

are on the menu, whichever is requisite.
Peace-Keeping Forces maintain the rhythm

of the global pulse. There will be a photo opportunity
so do not attempt to slap your camera

against the tinted window of the limousine.
There have been unwelcome comparisons

with the lens on the grill of the black maria. Excuse him.
He must now take his face to the Security Council.

Pause

You searched for quiet in spaces
between whistled starts,
between waves of what felt like tinnitus
rucked under your kapok-layered helmet.
The rattle of a kindly shower
had come at you from a freak angle.
There was a rumble that, from where
you lay, was only a rumour of a hum,
where metal wheels bass-pedalled the lines
a mile off, seemed to respond to the night flashes.

Your subliminal breath, loaded
with its own span of pain
cancelled words
you thought you were speaking,
but tripped a phone-echo,
undermined your own attempt
at a joke reply to the crepitation
in the headphones,
while the fox-bats kecked
at the tank-fumes.

II

78 RPM

O Mein Papa, foxtrots,
none of them measured up.
The vibrato of an irate joker, trebles
slipping through the fog of static,
an oboe quarrelling with hiss.
They were trying too hard to please.
Didn't change the needle, you could
play it with a thorn. The tiny tin box
of used pinpricks was a waste of space.
Winding down, an old man sobbed,
bogged in mud, hilariously
lockjawed. This was more like it.

They broke easily but the label
held the sharp-edged pieces. Shellac:
a dog nosing an ear-trumpet
revved to a dizzying soup. The arm,
lowered, was a bird pecking
on the warp of a glistening wave of oil.
Scratched, the regular click confirmed me
and when it faded I'd frisbee them
like clay pigeons, but had no gun
to shatter them over waste ground.
The Vienna Boys' Choir was stung
into silence in the nettle patch.

Langtree, April

A distant mower mows and mows.
This churchyard: gravestones uniformly grey,
sacred to the memory,
some round-topped, some square.
The mower falls silent, flies buzz, it starts up again.
Primroses, buttercups at my feet.
Throaty crows are having complex arguments above my head.
I wrote a poem about ravens once but it says nothing.
I have nothing to say about these crows.
I like the way gravestones begin over time to lean.
They fall out of line with their fellows,
the taller ones in particular,
a ragged community with the yew and holly overshading,
and rooks have streaked some with their white shit.
It feels peaceful here in spite of peacocks' screams
from The Old Rectory, tractors in busy fields,
wheel-whispers on the main road up the hill behind me.
Sunbeams angle brilliantly but the light breeze is chill.
Horse-clops, women talking equine lore,
a large dog bellows.
Church is locked, with warning signs, cameras.
The sluttish stones are kicking their heels.
Line up there, you 'orrible lot. Right dress!
A distant mower mows and mows.

First Woodpecker

His father pours it for him, testing him
in the webs and flaws of drink,
lifts him to tangled branches.

He learns to unscrew apple sheds,
fulcrum the bottle with both hands,
watches bubbles rise and spit

in his tumbler. Red cap, black cheek,
green wings, dagger beak build a nest
in his mind. The bottle's a conical shell

waiting for the snug breech. Brown glass
contains the stab and sparks in his throat,
sweet with the sweetness that clusters

around his heart, guts and bladder,
all the way to the tip of his penis.
He remembers forty years later

with a sudden, returning swoop:
the woodpecker creates waves
of forest air, grips bark,

gives a sarcastic peal of laughter:
everything after this can be okay.

Goldfinches

In my family there were always plenty of goldfinches.
Ma had to hire a man to disinfect
behind the hockey prints. Nevertheless,
we took turns feeding them with praise.
Washing the goldfinches was like giving birth:
first you must wipe them with a damp cloth;
then they are dried on Japanese rice paper.
I had a goldfinch once which I bought from the butcher.
It turned a mouldy green. I knew then
that there were real goldfinches such as the ones
my family had acquired in a principled way
and then there were fake which existed in the world.
My brothers knew more about goldfinches than I did
and would never impart the secrets of their brood
in case a burglar broke in and forced me to unleash
the secrets. Whenever I saw goldfinches
in sycamore trees I knew I would win
but goldfinches got tangled in the conversation
at meal-times. Uncle Paul said their song patterns
were proof that the earth was round like a coin.
Ma refused to talk about it and you could tell
she was thinking about gravitational pull
which crackled her nerves. The Rise of Mussolini,
Pa said, was caused by goldfinches. Nobody knew how many
goldfinches Pa had and sometimes he was absent
for long periods, making his goldfinch arrangements.

Musical Vienna – A Guided Tour

Into the toilets of the Albertina,
they pipe Mozart piano sonatas.
You emerge to wash in a pristine basin,
blushing at your mirrored face

as the attendant, alerted
by a triggered signal, reflushes,
and on departure, gives you a
look. Your strains descend

into the famous sewers – rats intercut
with zithering shadows – and on Mondays
at 16.00 it's possible to drop in.
The Harry Lime Tour, weather permitting,

and if no renovations are in progress,
will show you your Wolfgang-Johann
wheeling to the less-than-blue Danube,
transposed from keyboard to full orchestra.

Gothic Aunt Revival

They strode, manly cathedrals through side-streets,
imposing Ur-Goths. Wore, like furred copes,
the bodies of foxes with which as eager
girls they'd been blooded, draped around
their aisle-wide shoulders. Monkish, they'd eat
anything with a face, their own whiskered
like stained-glass window cats, kissed me
with powdered cheek-flesh, soft as a bishop's.
They served tea in Rockingham chalices
reciting their favourite psalms, nerves

like febrile lamps in long drawing-room naves.
Afficionados came from far in whining Morris Minors
to view those flying-buttress arms, their gargoyle
smiles that never took an answer for an answer,
their whispering transepts and triforium gallery hats,
their incense perfumes stifling a visitor's hymn
of adoration. These minsters would never,
like their country cousin churches, dissolve
in English showers. The dimmed chancels
of their spirits were always worth the detour.

Sheep and Poetry

Sheep are panting in the heat,
vibrations run through sausages of wool,
their ears narrow wing mirrors,
sides criss-crossed with blue dye.
They wear their shit like copious jewellery,

flick their heads as they inspect us
through the french windows.
The reader reads about her kitchen,
the tragic early death of her niece,
the imaginary friend she had.

Full grown lambs are the most curious,
stand on a step, poised.
Their mothers wander off, unimpressed
by pararhyme and grief. Infant
memories are less interesting than grass.

But the lambs jostle for position,
seem to like the one about the fish
in the clear water of a Cornish harbour,
how the poet drove his sleeping child
one long night through sleeping villages.

The Colour of Memory

walking across a field, an unarmed man.
One more step and there will be a blast.
I'm afraid to miss the moment:
an explosion, there's nothing I can do
nor can I turn away. A carrier
comes round the corner and
the shape disappears from sight.
I dream this scene a few times after that:
the man walking through a minefield,
a lone figure. It's summer when it happens,
sun flooding purple earth,
green smells of a nearby forest but I remember only
this black figure on a black field in Chechnya.

This black figure on a black field in Chechnya:
green smells of a nearby forest but I remember only
sun flooding purple earth.
A lone figure – it's summer when it happens –
the man walking through a minefield.
I dream this scene a few times after that:
the shape disappears from sight,
comes round the corner and
nor can I turn away. A carrier –
an explosion... there's nothing I can do,
I'm afraid to miss the moment;
one more step and there will be a blast.
Walking across a field, an unarmed man.

SHOSTAKOVICH 5

The applause riots for thirty-one minutes by the clock on the wall.
No-one staggers, faints or is bundled out to a body-crammed cell.

Tears like pepper vodka flow for a shy man on the podium who wears his suit
as if to shrug it off and disappear. This Baikal swell is the tidal opposite

of our stilled ovations for Koba (next to the clock) smiling, vast.
We are part of a movement we call spontaneity. Later, those lips twitched:

who organised the standing up? We roar as Mravinsky brandishes the score
above his head – we are no longer sane – slashes at *Pravda's* censure.

These chords' progressions have jinked bat-like into old rooms of the heart,
trapdoors fling open, where they dance, live discrete.

Rafah

The incident was looked into – look –
  no, let me – the incident was looked into
    and there is no evidence – no evidence – no–
      let me – no, she knowingly entered the forbidden –
        She knowingly. With a satchel, for God's sake.
          She knowingly and in full. Well obviously
            she was being used to lure soldiers.
            Under the rules of engage. Under the. Under the.
            Under the rules of engagement she may, she may, yes,
        be wounded, yes. Under the rules. She may.
      Yes, I know she was shot dead, that is what. Yes,
I know the satchel was shot, because it could so easily.
  It could so easily have had an explosive device.
      That is normal procedure for. And no-one, no not one,
        can explain what she was doing in the forbidden zone.
        So I don't think. Shed tears for.
          Look. That is what. Is being. Is being.
            Looked in– Cleared already? The Unit
          Commander has come under very heavy
        fire for his decision. Yes, I know he was cleared but.
      I know some soldiers are complaining,
    some soldiers are always.
    Thirteen times? Look, there was
clear evidence she was carrying a bomb.
    Suicide bombers are getting younger
        every day, so. No, no, wait, he turned away,
           but then, thinking she might still be alive
              and a very real threat –
                no well you say she was already shot three times
                  and then he switched his rifle to automatic

and fired thirteen shots into her,
in fact it was ten. "He emptied his
clip into her?!" No, that is what. No, that is what.
Is being looked into. And I have no doubt.
I have no doubt. That we shall find. That –
no let me finish. No. That we shall. Find.

Kafka's Recipe for Boiled Cabbage

First you must obtain a permit for the possession of a cabbage.
Go at once to the authorities and wait in line.
After many days, you may see an official.
It will be completely useless to explain you have come for
    a cabbage permit,
he will not understand you, will be astonished at your
    impertinence,
may put you under arrest, may have you incarcerated for
    your own safety.

Even if he does not do this and actually grants you a permit
    to own a cabbage,
which is extremely rare, if not practically unheard of,
you would still have to apply for permission to enter your
    kitchen.
Your housekeeper would probably prevent you from so doing.
She certainly won't understand your intentions and report
    you to the Police
who will certainly arrest you and have you incarcerated.

Even if this does not happen and you effect an entrance into
    the kitchen
to boil your cabbage, which is extremely rare if not practically
    unheard of,
you cannot assume that the cooker will be working.
It will certainly be out of order, in which case it will be
    necessary to apply
to the appropriate authorities for a supply of gas. This will
    take months
to obtain and may result in your arrest and incarceration.

Even if this does not happen, and you obtain a gas permit,
which is completely unheard of and has never been done
> by anyone,
you may ignite the gas and place a saucepan of water on
> it to boil.
In order to prepare the cabbage you will need a sharp knife.
For this you will need to apply to the appropriate authorities
who will certainly arrest you for intent to possess a dangerous
> weapon.

In prison, you must wait in line to be served some boiled
> cabbage.
But there is no guarantee that you will be permitted to eat it.
The boiled cabbage may be taken away from you at any time.

Vote Pine Tree

Still evergreen, alive with resin.
Bark is thin and scaly, branches tight,
four thousand years of life in spite of toxins.

Spring shoots are candles affirming
the soil's fertility and the vigour
of my delving roots. Seeds wing
from cones, dispersed by wind and birds
whose excrement feeds their sprouting birth.

I gave you a harvest of campaign posters
so you'd remember my face, my pine-skirts
when you saw them on the ballot paper.
You liked my father's straightness too.

I was not elected, though your purpled thumbs
amassed forests that climb mountains.

Vote Horse

True men dream of owning me, so I count
on your thumbs to elect me President
of Afghanistan. I am stronger than the opium
you grow, will drug you with my promises
of speed and food. Tether me with steel, lash
me, I am never tamed. My electric eyes abolish
the nights of cowering invaders. I gallop all over
the North to bring you roads and generators.

I'm destined to return to Abraham's bosom.
The Koran praises me – *stalwart desert skimmer* –
triumphed in Operation Enduring Freedom,
I drove out terror with Terror. Uzbeks swear
my laugh has sent evil-doers back to God.
No mountain path defeats me. Stand aside.

Lord Hutton reports

I am satisfied that this is not a case
in which the Crown could have had any knowledge
that a notoriously unstable egg would hurl itself
from the wall it was ill-advised enough to sit on.

I am further satisfied that subconsciously
the King's horses and indeed the King's men
may have wished to reassure the Crown
that the position of Mr Dumpty was perfectly safe,

but there is absolutely no evidence whatsoever
to suggest that the so-called "Dumpty Dossier",
now in the public domain, overstressed
the stability of the egg's position in any particular.

Turning now to Miss Liddell,
who obtained an interview with Mr Dumpty,
which he was not authorised to give, just prior
to his fall: the vast bulk of the evidence

laid before me states categorically that it was
this very interview that destabilised him. For years
a loyal servant of the royal household,
this extremely able ovoid was put under intolerable pressure,

in particular by Miss Liddell's persistent and intrusive
line of questioning. Clearly, much needs to be done
in refining procedures for press interviews with leaking eggs.

In conclusion, the cavalry is to be commended
for its efforts, which went well beyond its duty of care,
to reassemble Mr Dumpty.

R&R

This is the fortnight I ride the subway
to the flat-ends of the sprawl, two hundred
miles of metal. I've hassled to the front
of car 1, hands flat against palm-warm glass.
The train smashes through darkness, straw people
sit on local platforms staring nowhere,
a jarred look they've perfected in stale bars.
My body tacks with the whipping stretches.
The squeal is a nostalgic pleasure: hurt
victim of a curve. There's so much iron
in the scorch of those sways I'm a flung kid
getting the taste of the new Dinky toy
I loved to suck on. Workmen sway lanterns
along buddleia sidings. I keep watch
for sewer rats but see only shadows.
Then the express stations, the berserk brakes,
figures graded like refugees. They come
bagging into space, wing to the handholds,
miss them, inch their way in, are swiftly penned,
looking out past the crowded heads with that
honed disregard that is something of me.

Shades

                  don't walk, they slink or they sidle.
Those in their second six months, the deacons,
shamble but must play it with humility. Only the dukes,
who are about to be demobbed, swalter, their
heels scraping the floor. If a shade walks like that
in training he can expect a good slackering.
A shade keeps hands out of pockets, or deacons
fill them with sand and sew them up. The sand
chags the groin and weeps impetigo. Show respect
to deacons, grandads and dukes or get skelted
in the bird parlour. Talk loud, lie on your bed
in the daytime you'll be frotted into next week.
Turn down the rim of your boots, leave your top
button undone, tip your cap to one side, don't do
your belt up tightly enough, you'll be ponied so
hard you'll forget your name. Every grandad has
his own shade who he can of course pony. You can
complain to your grandad if someone else ponies you.
Your grandad may pony that person. A shade must
sneck up dosh, bacca and choff for his own
grandad – he can ignore anyone else's shouts.
The only exception is a grandad who is stronger
than yours. But there is none of this in our regiment.

Chapter VII

The love-making of crocodiles
   takes place under
the sludge-dark water. They warble,
splatter and rub the undersides
of yellow-white jaws while spearhead
    whip-tails flounder.

She elevates her head, they nudge
   with questing snouts,
he strokes her body's roughcast ridge
with both forelegs. They arch their backs,
blow bubbles, play games of twinesnake,
   then with half-shut

eyes, he surveys her, positions
   her with webbed feet
and mounts. Buoyant copulation
lasts for fifteen minutes. She lays
her eggs in sand some yards away,
   well out of sight.

The lovemaking of turtles takes
   place off the shore
of their birth. They've found their way back
over one thousand five hundred
miles, navigated the sun's road,
   by earth's threadbare

magnetic field. The males cruise, stir,
   quarrel over
arriving females. The victor
bites her shell, clasps her carapace
with his flippers. He forces her
   down, she hovers,

sinks, strives to rise to breathe the air.
   They play and plough
the water for six tumbling hours,
till the male breaks off to patrol,
but she must climb her domicile,
   the beach, to lay.

The love-making of humans takes
   place deep among
a field of straggling charlock
whose petals fleck them with mustard,
or in the woods kissed by bistort.
   Birth is in Spring.

Owls

They perch in their dripping cages
to the left of the occupied castle,
between the rhododendron walk
and the merchandising outlet.

They have converted motionlessness
into owl-stillness. Their vests of down,
massy under speckled camouflage,
shield them against the English chill.

As the long nights fall, rustlings
in nearby leaf-carpets alert them
only to their jail. Their plumage ruffles
as fat as bombers' overcoats.

A clank of bucket. Albino mice corpses
rot on blood-filmed trays. The bearded
and the hooded close their eyes and see,
but no longer seek, attack-proof caves.

At the flying display, the keeper mentions
they've been trapped in Waziristan,
enticing them back and forth
with morsels of fresh-killed rabbit.

Sleeper Cell

He's a gentleman, but keep an eye on his garden shed
supplied and built by squads of men who do not sleep. Askance,
observe him forsake his grey mobile, then return to shade
his sky-light from periscopes. Over the wattle back-fence

bring the chat around to your new photos of the simoom.
This is a mind that skewers the grammar of the lock-up,
takes his polite children to visit inner-city farms,
fishes *The Secrets of the Self* out of his neighbour's skip.

A subject in a raincoat lined with faded purple gauze
can't be monitored too sedulously. Note the lesson
behind llama eye-lashes: how, on blatant Saturdays,
he looks like you, looking at him. Forage, learn to listen

for his sermons to the pigeons behind Tesco Local.
A personage who may justify the laziest qualms
of the concierge, may also hack his way through firewalls,
unmask his own brand of menace in immigrant chatrooms.

TED SMITH

See how the Bloody Tower has been reassembled
seamlessly by Spanish engineers. The White Tower
was also conveyed, flint by flint, to a new location

on Hampstead Heath, overlooking the flooded city.
Forty thousand tons of stonework were transported
by gantries specially designed by Libyan masons.

HGVs from the Sudan were used to carry
the battlements. A rust-eaten sceptre is in a museum
in Baku, taken there by Armenian gemmologists,

with two stuffed ravens. Beware of displaced beggars
from Tower Hamlets who hang around Traitor's Gate.
You can view life-sized replicas of Beefeaters

in The Museum of Conflict Resolution, Marrakesh.
The Spaniards Inn is a good place for a lunch break.
While you're here you might like to visit Highgate

Cemetery, say hello to Karl Mark and other famous
painters but keep your u-pods out of sight of the locals.
These towers are called Ted Smith after the boy who led

Fijian archaeologists to the site. All they found at first
was a machicoulis protruding from Lake Thames.

III

Recruitment

Be aware of the empty seat before the otherwise panel,
the slide of the elbow off the table of although,
the meanwhile stitching in the uniform,
the set of black swerves on the tarmac of whether or not.

The pit-bull is loose in the certainly parade ground,
muzzle loosely fastened with ifs.
A downpour of shadows is breaking through
your howsoever mess-room window.

So make your peace with the tank of notwithstanding,
the armoured car that splatters forthwith from its tracks
and never have sex with nevertheless.

Cellar

This terrace was built on a stream.
When rain falls it oozes through bricks
in the outer wall. The concrete floor has
crumbled into flakes that scuff your shoes.

Once-vicious hooks collapse from mortar
when you tug them lightly, rust staining
fingers a deep indelible amber. You'd
hesitate before pulling that tangle of wire.

In worm-holed joists an inch above
head-height a newspaper the colour of tea
has been stuck, a *Daily Telegraph*
from 1894 – headlined Trouble In Belfast.

The dividing wall balances the house,
under whose floor you're a velvet mole.
Soggy-dried cardboard instructions:
Official Bomb Shelter: For The Protection

Of Twenty People. Breathing in air sharp
with compost, you scent diseases long since
banished, creeping back. You mount
rotting wooden steps with chilled feet,

the cellar on you like the secrets you forgot
to keep, the photo-negatives itching in the drawer,
the way your lover's sleeping sigh
turns you to watch him on the pillow.

Tourist Bus Halt

The mud-boiling face of the river, fragile
boats piled with mint, the rudiments of trees
and the monkeys adroit as silica
have become Sri Lanka. By a kitchenette,
striped green cushions of water-melons.
A man sits, dreaming, and I ask myself
who plays this man? Who animates his pretty,
quiet wife? Their agents must bid on behalf
of their charmingly filthy children,
and the unnecessary diseases they die from
will be cured or prevented somehow.
Nothing sleeps unless sleep is part of the backstory.
The way that loin-clothed beggar extends
his wand of an arm must give way to aura.
At the heart of the rectangle, he's ours.
The gut-strewn dog in the ditch will gift
its pixellation to pull-back shots. The egrets
that settle with grace on the cattle are already
January on your calendar. Here I am in zoom,
my roseola at the disposal of foreground.
The clouds are translating in fast forward,
in time-lapse, in anything but the awkward
skies. The loin-cloth, the melon-seller know
and they've surrendered. But look at the egrets,
their feathers have not been trafficked
as they flap, indolent in the haze.

Rehearsing The Anopheles Play

You sense her warmth, quiver. Only
females drink blood, carry its weight
in the abdomen like pregnancy. Bite –
without hurting – just a smidgen

through your palps, let's see the furry teeth
and now you inflate yourself. You're heavy
but flit adroitly. Victim: hone your sweating
skills, think anaemic, ache your muscles.

We'll work on the nausea. Make up
your yellow face, let's *feel* the jaundice.
Be economical with fits from kidney
failure, rein in the leg spasm. Coma

is a tough customer: a mobile stillness.
Doctor, please: stethoscope in right hand.
Listen to heart, roll eyes once only,
take blood pressure. Mime open cupboard –

shake head: no medicine. Not too emphatic,
more a tic, an absent-minded melancholy
and exit, you have other patients.
Mosquito, this is your re-entry cue

the audience should fear your hum.

In A Supply Tunnel, Rafah

Once he's in the air, upside down,
he clings to the stem
on which he blossoms.
They right him, lower him into the pit.
Cartons of chocolate,
Egyptian cigarettes block out sky,
thump and bounce near his feet.
The goat which has lived
as it would shrivel, by its own laws,
comes down in jerks,
strapped, head-bagged.
Hooves dig as nerves riot
at the passage entrance.
They had said keep moving ahead of it,
tug and tug, it will come after.
He inhales damp sand air,
eyes the warped uprights,
the belly-sag in the roof struts.
The head in the jute sack tosses, snorts,
until the boy wins the battle of animal wills.
His head-torch lights passageways
to five different routes,
some blasted to blockage.
He chooses the chalked arrow, approaches,
sees the white chink ahead expand to a square.
His arms protest from the haul,
half-squashed cartons, the bleating shape.
He stands in the depths of the pit, chest heaves
as if giving birth, no word to throw upwards,

hands blistered by the rope,
the sacked head quieter now in sensed light.
He waits on a dangled harness.

Flight

The air-convoy over-passes the foothills of the Kush stirring concentric eddies of dust. I fend off the needles of grit as the windblast tears at my patou, below is the meltwater-river Kunar, above me the bang and flutter of blades. In heat-mist the voice of Sir Mortimer Durand: *the vexed question of where the border should be set*. I snatch at my unwinding turban. If they had water and a mill all this land could be cultivated, but there's no rain, there is nothing. Darius leading his caravans, the ruins of the White Huns. I can see – and don't see – in a Saudi living room a fossil and a palaeolithic tool, a pebble carved with a laurel-crowned head. By a hutment, a beetle boy lifts a bale of sticks, hoists it onto his back. The tribes that settled in the Desert of Ghor called themselves the Ban-Afghani. In the Year Of The Mouse, 1396, Timur visited the shrine of the dervish Baba Sanga at Andkhoy, who cast a raw sheep-breast at the Lord of the Fortunate Conjunction. Allah had ordained that he should take Khorasan, also named The Breast, The Heart of the World. The lower slopes are stubbled walnut and pine stumps cut long ago. An American complains, *Combat is the devil's game. That's why our prayers aren't answered – only Satan listens*. Poppies planted well away from the road. Children being taught under the shade of a plum tree. As Alexander pressed on he found the regions of Sogdiana and Bactria hostile. I see and do not see ten years of explosives as yet unearthed by trained detectorists in a slur of landscape. The road is punctuated by wreckage, statements that refuse debate. Alexander's sergeants can't curb drunkenness, have to write widows fictional letters, can't tell them their husbands split their skulls falling into a ditch. Crumbled masonry, teeth-walls of gaping homes grin, slip away beneath my feet, Taliban stride through halls, whips in their hands, pronounce smooth faces worthy of death, wolves howl up in the peaks, mountain lions creep through the forward operating bases looking for food.

Some Useful Phrases

I have run out of petrol. Good evening.
A slaty storm-frown gathers on the Hindu Kush.
How are you? Sticky warmth fills the room.
I am hungry. I am twenty-three. Pleased to meet
you. It is hot but the summer ought to have left
six weeks ago. *Water is the main difficulty*
of such a journey as sufferers from syphilis
of the throat are apt to spit in the wells.

The road to Kabul is closed and in any case
I have run out of petrol. Drop your weapon.
Please. May I look at it? *There is the sound*
of partridges clucking. God is Great. Take
six paces forward. Take cognisance. Take five.
Put your hands on the fridge. How much is that?

Sniffer Patrol

Under New South Wales law, "a dog's nose is no more than an extension of a police officer."

Straight to it. I've chased
along scent maps lost to you.
I've traced the warm slick
of your guilt. They're
all banked. I've pawed them.

Reek calls through the dust and spook
of the funnelled crowd
as it heists through the tight street,
can't escape my handled trot.
I'm fledged and led by a relish
that nudges me back and forth.

In the cellars of the dark,
rotten bones tang me,
rouse my curbed chew,
my sprinkle of nose-dew, the thrill
in my belly, sneeze
of muzzle. Stale marrow
is refined, renewed in me.
I truffle the decades.

I can taste all the routes to my truth,
they steal it out of a tic of fur
and convict with a scratch
of my pad. In line-ups
I've yapped a pair of dirty shoes
to solitary.

Camp X-Ray

The unborn children sail into the bay in cutters
loaded with bottles of spirulina. They list to starboard
when the guards show up but hold their ground
in the offing, well beyond the razor wire.

The sky is void of egrets
that used to hover like drones.
The emptiness of the air panics me.
The unborn children have come with their petition,

may swing open my door with digital remotes
but I don't negotiate for my release,
I've projects to complete.
I open my lids – an after-image degrades –

to the hill where ravens, their feathers wind-twitched,
mass, quarelling blotches
of redacted documents.
A thickness in my cage congregates.

The Restroom

Running off this corridor, on the left, is a row of nine small cells, each 3 ft by 7 ft, with a prisoner in each. At the end of the corridor are two offices, a restroom for the torturers, and a computer room.

tattered back numbers on Ercol table

        tea in aluminium pot
dark, acidic
                half-lemon
knife on saucer near hob

    when button's pressed

  coffee-machine hiccups beige
liquid

    Van Gogh's Boots hangs on the wall

air smells of patchouli joss-stick
                on carpet
a trodden digestive

        kitchen roll unwinds

a notice
    please clean up after yourself.

Medical Advances

Feet should be well above head,
bench four by seven,
cloth placed over eyes and brow.

In a controlled manner, water is applied
to cloth and lowered until it covers
both nose and mouth, air-flow restricted

for twenty to forty seconds due to presence
of cloth, water applied continuously
from height of twelve to twenty-four inches.

After this period, cloth is lifted,
individual allowed to breathe unimpeded
for three or four full intakes.

Procedure may be repeated.
Water is usually applied from a cup
or small watering can with spout.

This procedure has raised our awareness
of hypo-thermic shock: if cooling is rapid
survival is more likely. An ice-cold saline
solution lowers temperature of brain, which
can function without oxygen. Once surgery
is complete, warm blood can be pumped in.
There are implications for face transplants.

Waiting for the Americans

After Cavafy

Why are we all assembled and waiting?
It is the Americans; they will be here today.

Why is nothing being done in the presidential palaces?
Why are the generals being briefed, but not making decisions?
Because the Americans are coming
and they will give us the benefit of their advice.

Why is the president getting up so early? Why does he
recline in his marble bath with its golden taps,
washing his formidable body and smiling?
Because he is preparing to receive the US generals
and he has listed many names with their ranks.

Why have the Weapons Inspectors forgathered
in their tropical suits and name tags?
Why have they climbed into Humvees
and crossed the desert to a neutral country?
Why are they taking home their report?
Why will no-one study their recommendations?

And why don't the newspapermen emerge
from The Orient Gate Hotel to interview the wounded?
Why has the city emptied so quickly,
why are people entering makeshift shelters?

It is night and the Americans are not here yet.
But they will come, soon.

The Agony

We eat, drink, sleep drone-relateds,
the agony is dense, graphic
and proportionate.
Personal objections *were* expressed
to some Agency colleagues
about chair-use and water.
Music and other allegations
were not real information
when we searched them,
all of them open, verifiable,
also they were generated
in a different sector of the Agency.
An interview we gave in 2006
revisited saved-lives outcomes
through enhanced intel,
which consequently came out
clear and prismatic.
The Black Site e-mails were convincing
and in the area of shock,
absolutely above board.
That report was down-graded
so that agony levels were into Code Pink.
Therefore we were the principal
architect of the 50 page legal opinion
on Abductives which was flagged up
as standard value-added
for the latter half of 2007.
That was after responsive agonies
in the chain of command. And
we have now retreated from the view

that abductional was not renditional
although renditioning is less
jeopardous than pre-2010. Whereas,
an enhanced and subsequent interrogative,
which High-Ups refused to release,
included removing US citizens. We may
have activated those tendencies.
The agony of looking into that
will be forceful, but unconfirmed
wedding kills are not who we are.

Imminent Release

When news came he would walk in a month,
they brought him burgers, french fries,
peanut and jelly sandwiches.

They broke routine to watch him eat,
see him contemplate
his belly's coy expansion.

When he threw up they roared –
result! – left him to the sour gruel.
He retreated into his corner.

Later, he hung out with ranks of platters. They coaxed:
we need that you look good to go. In that last week
he was surrounded by congealed forcemeat,

dried pap, stony fries. Shadow patches
of flies seethed. He wondered
if the sesame seeds he'd picked from buns

and planted, would grow in the sand.
The three-piece they put him in fell in folds.
On his step up to the paddy wagon:

Welcome to the terror-watchlist.
Peace out, dawg.

The Trojan Enquiry

Was there ever a threat of aggression from Troy?

All the pertinent intelligence said there was.

Which you plagiarised, then sexed up. Is that not true?

I stand by every word. We did not dramatise.

Should we have given them time to return Helen?

The Ravage Inspectors had sounded the alarm.

You read the Peace Dossier from Agamemnon?

I'd heard it was dodgy from hoplites in his team.

Were there any pressures on the defence budget?

No. Urgent Ship Requirements went through very fast.

And sword, shield and spear-makers never overcharged?

No request was ever ruled out on grounds of cost.

Was there firm intel guiding conduct of the siege?

Yes, it came from disaffected slaves of Priam.

Was that adequate basis on which to engage?

We did not know it was defective at the time.

Whose responsibility was the Trojan Horse?

The decision was taken in full Cabinet.

Weren't your plans compromised by Cassandra's outburst?

The change in our strategy was proportionate.

How can you defend the subsequent massacre?

We were confronted with a vile dictatorship.

And it would be hard to return to Ithaca?

That was not my remit. A storm in a teacup.

Camp No

I did see guards hand over
someone in a dog cage.
The van was backed up,
doors open. When I asked,
the reply was: delivering pizza.

There were rumours of walling.
I heard the muffled noises.
Then the sudden absences in June.
The enquiry confirmed
that it was simultaneous suicides:
taking their own lives was a PR move.

A statement was issued:
hunger strike is an asymmetrical
act of warfare waged against us.
They're offered tube-fed chocolate,
strawberry or vanilla –
the choice is theirs.
They sometimes say No.
But the outcome is the same.

LEADER

If the forebrain of a minnow is removed
it sees, eats, swims like any normal fish
but lacks hesitancy, doesn't mind

leaving the glitter of the shoal which,
even when the group wants to advance,
turns to see if fins, gills, eyes are behind

and lets itself be guided by the movement
of the whole, while the brainless minnow
will dart forward and the shoal follow quickly.

Orange

Despite various citric acts
officials warned it was far too early
to locate the causes of these bright orange trees.
In Nahr-e Saraj, one of the concentrated areas,
lemons are affected by orange policy,
yet measures have been taken. This
particular one was exactly as planted.
It displaced six others and it was either
a blood-orange or of similar early-fruiting-type
to the lemon. Growers insist on a patrol-base
and lemon security is handled seriously.
Downing St issued a white on black statement
which promises that our involvement
will soon be on the ground. However oranges
north of the orange areas are at the heart
of the relationship which is part of the process:
these steps are a backward step when so much
depends on trust. The ratio of lime-green
to dark-blue oranges this year have been scheduled
to affect the withdrawal, but it remains
to be seen. Next of lemon kin have been numbered
but it is not known how many oranges
are in fact in existence. The Dept is considering
its response to orange health:
it is thought to be safe in the majority
of fruits if peeled by yourself.
A spokesman admitted the peeling season
was to blame for a lot of orange blossom
but that canned segments would be
the norm in future. Seeds have been sown.

Elegy

Give peace in our time and you soon discover
armed neutrality doesn't come cheap. Too wise
to govern the world we shall politely own
the places that are left. Still, insolence
must be put down. You know my method.
It is founded upon the patting of heads
by smooth hands. But far too often
these days peace means feeding the mouth
that bites you. Or look at it this way:
peace is an impermanent fad; if we lose
this war, I'll start another in my wife's name.
Peace is a room in which it's safe to eat muffins.
My peace I leave with you, you can have it.
On certain conditions. Well, my kiss of peace.
These facts are worse than dreams of war.
The English seem to have no stomach
for this fight so let them understand the world
moves aside for him who knows where
he's going. We have to distrust each other,
it's our only defence against bomber-vests.
Other nations use force, we Britons use might
since peace is usually received in a hostile
spirit as if it were more dangerous than force.
The bonfire of hostilities is a high price to pay
when the cost is eternal espionage. Ignorance
of freedom is no excuse, it's the real thing.
I shall have more to say when I am dead.

Acknowledgements

Many thanks are due to the editors of the following magazines in which these poems, or versions of them, first appeared: *Blackbox Manifold, The Bow-wow Shop, The Delinquent, Envoi, Ink Sweat & Tears, The Interpreter's House, Magma, Other Poetry, Poetry Ireland Review, Poetry News, Poetry Proper, The Rialto, THE SHOp, Smith's Knoll, Stand, Under The Radar.*

'78 rpm' appeared in the anthology, *The Best of British Poetry 2011* (Salt) and 'Lord Hutton's Report' appeared in the anthology *Stripe* (Templar).

'Guided Tour' was placed in The Troubadour Poetry Competition; 'Saddam Hussein's Overbite Speaks' won second prize in the William Soutar Competition; 'The Colour of Memory' won first prize in the Ver Poets Competition; 'Rafah' won joint third prize in The Iraq Occupation Focus Poetry Competition; 'Ted Smith' won third prize in the Keats-Shelley Memorial Poetry Competition; 'The Agony' won first prize in the Essex Poetry Competition; 'Flight' was placed in the Torbay Poetry Competition.

For close reading and valuable comments very many thanks to: Delphine Breese-Laughran, Judy Brown, Jane Commane, Martyn Crucefix, Graham Fawcett, Phil Ruthen, Sound Crew, Greta Stoddart, Maggie Sullivan.

Acknowledgements of Sources

'From The Golfcart' (first six lines) – Konrad Lorenz: *On Aggression*. (Bantam).
'Ways to Build a Roadblock' – based on a passage from Ryzsard Kapuscinski: *Another Day of Life* (Penguin).
'Guided Tour' – adapted from *The Guardian*.
'The Trojan Enquiry' – The Chilcott Enquiry in stichomythia.
'Babur's Tulips' – Babur identifying 33 varieties is mentioned in Hamida Ghafour: *The Sleeping Buddha* (Constable).
'Like dense cotton and it started to burn' – the title quote is from a victim of phosphorus shell attacks during Operation Cast Lead and further details are from *The Guardian*.
'Shostakovich 5' – Ian McDonald: *The New Shostakovich*. Pimlico.
'Rafah' – derived from *The Guardian*
'R&R' – an argument with a passage from Don Delillo: *Libra* (Penguin).
'Flight' – an amalgam of various historical sources.
'Some Useful Phrases' – lines in italics are taken from Eric Newby: *A Short Walk in the Hindu Kush* (Picador).
'Medical Advances' – from *The Guardian* and others
'Waiting for the Americans' – after C. P. Cavafy: *Waiting for the Barbarians. The Collected Poems* (Oxford).
'Camp No': "Walling" is the practice of placing victim's heels close to wall and slamming the body against it. (Wikipedia)
'Leader' – adapted from Konrad Lorenz: *On Aggression* (Bantam).
'Elegy' – an amalgam of quotations and misquotations (Wordsworth Editions).